PRINCESSES, MERMAIDS &UNICORNS

ACTIVITY BOOK

Illustrated
Irina
Smirnova

TONS OF FUN ACTIVITIES!

CLEVER
Publishing

This book belongs to:

_____

_____

Three little mermaids are playing in the ocean. Color the longest of all the mermaid tails red. Color the second longest tail green, and color the shortest tail blue.

These fairy costumes have lost their wings!
Can you match them up?

Connect the dots and you will find what fell out of a fairy's bag. Do you know what it is?

Seven princesses mixed up their dancing shoes. Draw a line that connects one shoe in each pair to the other.

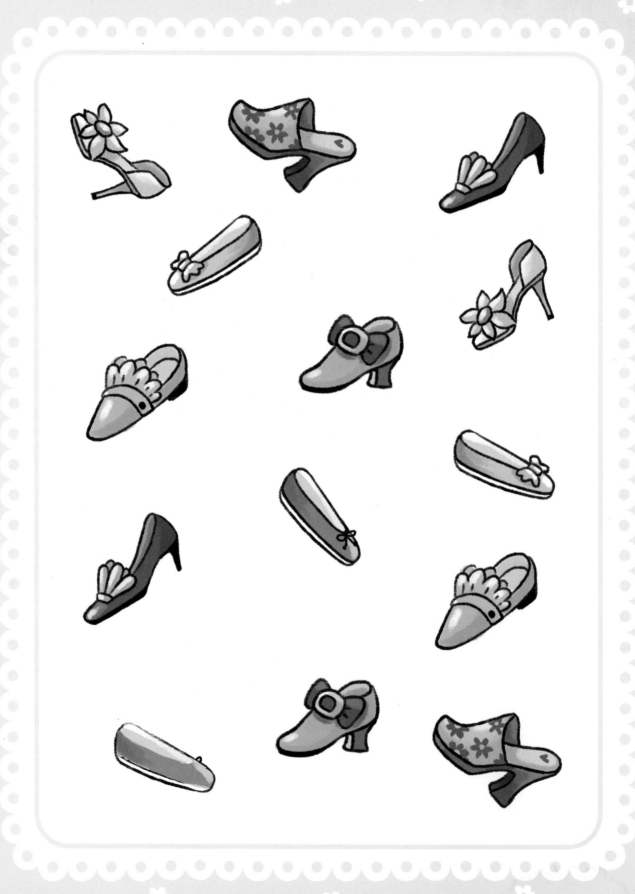

Find the white skirts and socks in this picture and color them.

Color each fairy's wings.

Only one of these vines leads to the fairy's flower petal home. Trace a path to guide her there.

START

FINISH

Help this princess get ready for the ball by coloring her dress as carefully as you can.

What comes next? Draw the items needed to repeat each pattern.

Find the shadow that belongs to this fairy.

Find a clear path to get this princess safely to her carriage.

Draw a beautiful princess here.

Choose a handbag for each princess that will match her gown. Then color them in.

Can you spot six differences between these pictures?

Complete this picture by drawing the right side of the castle.

You're invited to a royal ball—but you can only carry a small handbag. Color two items that you would bring in your purse.

Draw some beautiful gemstones and ornaments on this crown to help decorate it for a princess.

Color this ballerina using the colors shown below her.

This ballerina looks lost. Help her find a path to the stage.

STAGE →

START

FINISH

Find the matching halves of each picture and join them with a line.

The princess who lives in this room has misplaced her teddy bears. How many can you find?

Welcome to Fairyland!
Color the picture and
find three crowns, four
butterflies, two birds
and five handbags.

Connect the dots to meet one princess's favorite pet.

Draw a face for each princess.

The frames hanging in this princess's bedroom are blank. Can you draw her some pictures?

Spot the differences between these pictures.

Draw and color the right side of each picture.

Draw a line to show where each missing
piece of the stage belongs.

Find four fairies as you color this picture.

Draw and color the missing butterfly wings and flower petals in this meadow.

What will you name the royal unicorn? Color this magical picture of a princess and her pet.

This princess picked five beautiful roses and tied them together with a very long ribbon. Find and color her bouquet.

What beautiful ballerinas! Draw patterns on their dresses and color them in.

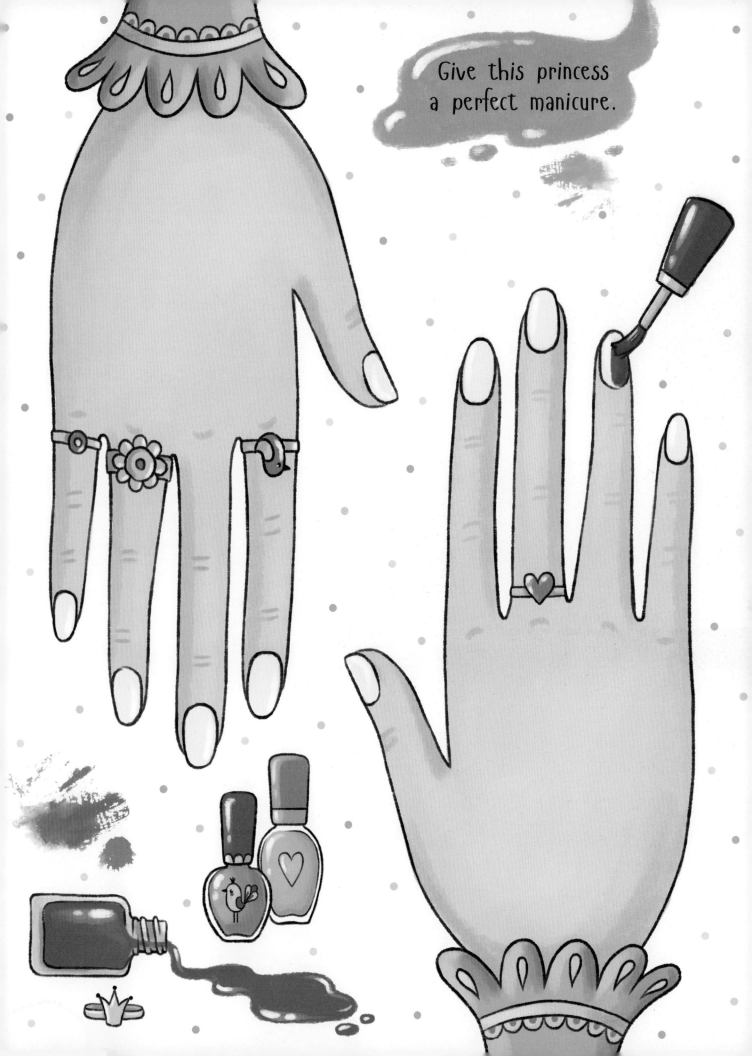

Give this princess a perfect manicure.

Draw some elegant hairstyles
for these little princesses
and color them in.

Decorate this
princess's carriage.

One prince is too shy
to give his flowers
to a princess.

Find the prince who's hiding and color him in.

Color these castles, giving each
one its own unique style.

Do the white flowers on this tree need some color? You decide.

There isn't much to eat at this tea party. Draw some extra treats for these princesses.

This is where the princess leaves her crown. Can you draw it on the table?

Find the fairies who are twins and color their dresses to make them match.

Draw yourself in a princess costume.